EVERY GENERATION NEEDS CARETAKERS

Abhijit Naskar is the twenty-first century mind of science, whose seminal philosophical touch has enabled modern Neuroscience to effectively engage in the human society towards diminishing the ever-growing conflicts among religions. As an untiring advocate of global harmony and peace, he became a beloved best-selling author all over the world with his very first book "The Art of Neuroscience in Everything". With various of his pioneering ventures into the Neuropsychology of religious sentiments, he has hugely contributed in the eradication of religious differences in our world, for which he is popularly hailed as a humanitarian neuroscientist, who takes the human civilization in the path of sweet general harmony.

EVERY GENERATION NEEDS CARETAKERS

THE GOSPEL OF PATRIOTISM

ABHIJIT NASKAR

Also by Abhijit Naskar

The Art of Neuroscience in Everything
Your Own Neuron: A Tour of Your Psychic Brain
The God Parasite: Revelation of Neuroscience
The Spirituality Engine
Love Sutra: The Neuroscientific Manual of Love
Homo: A Brief History of Consciousness
Neurosutra: The Abhijit Naskar Collection
Autobiography of God: Biopsy of A Cognitive Reality
Biopsy of Religions: Neuroanalysis towards Universal
Tolerance
Prescription: Treating India's Soul
What is Mind?
In Search of Divinity: Journey to The Kingdom of Conscience
Love, God & Neurons: Memoir of a scientist who found
himself by getting lost
The Islamophobic Civilization: Voyage of Acceptance
Neurons of Jesus: Mind of A Teacher, Spouse & Thinker
Neurons, Oxygen & Nanak
The Education Decree
Principia Humanitas
The Krishna Cancer
Rowdy Buddha: The First Sapiens
We Are All Black: A Treatise on Racism
The Bengal Tigress: A Treatise on Gender Equality
Either Civilized or Phobic: A Treatise on Homosexuality
Wise Mating: A Treatise on Monogamy
Illusion of Religion: A Treatise on Religious
Fundamentalism
The Film Testament
Human Making Is Our Mission: A Treatise on Parenting
I Am The Thread: My Mission
7 Billion Gods: Humans Above All
Lord is My Sheep: Gospel of Human
Morality Absolute
A Push in Perception
Let The Poor Be Your God
Conscience over Nonsense
Saint of The Sapiens
Time to Save Medicine
Fabric of Humanity

Build Bridges not Walls: In the name of Americana
The Constitution of The United Peoples of Earth
Lives to Serve Before I Sleep
When Humans Unite: Making A World Without Borders
All For Acceptance
Monk Meets World
Mission Reality
Citizens of Peace: Beyond The Savagery of Sovereignty
Operation Justice: To Make A Society That Needs No Law
See No Gender
The Gospel of Technology

*To You, who has figured out
that you and I are one*

CONTENTS

Worth of A Human

What is the point of you? What is your worth? And by worth I am not talking about your financial value, I am talking about something much more significant than that. So, I ask again - what is your worth? And you won't find the answer in any scripture or church - you won't find it even in this book. Because no external power can give you the answer to something so incredibly existential in nature.

If you want to know your worth, ask yourself, what are you without your bank account. The worth of a person lies in character. The same goes for a nation and the same goes for a world. Therefore, a nation's worth lies not in the value of its currency, but in the character of its people. And it all begins with the individual - it all begins with you. Your character holds not just the worth of your own life, but that of the lives of your people as well. So, feel like it's the feeling of your society and act like it's the action of your society.

But mark you, here I do not mean, feeling and acting like the society, rather, I am asking you to feel, think and act as an original, brave and conscientious human being, so that you become the very emblem of humanhood in front of others, for them to draw their life's inspiration from. Doing what the society wants, makes you a second hand human - wanting the society to do what you want, makes you a narcissistic bigot - but being an embodiment of humanhood without any expectation from others, is what makes you a sentient human.

However, what you must also keep in mind that nobody is immune to social conditioning or social programming. Everybody is vulnerable to it - to the pressure of the society. That's why it is biologically impossible to have no expectation from the society, no matter how subtle. But the question is why? Why do we crave for acceptance from the society? Why do we expect approval of the society in everything we do.

Unless a person has some sort of pathological condition that makes them unable to create a healthy bond between the self and the society, everybody has the urge for being accepted by the society, by the community, by the environment – to look for approval from others. So, what is the reason that we look for approval from others - from the people around us?

The reason is that we are not wired to be loners. We are social animals. Being in a community makes us stronger. And that's the faculty that actually enabled our ancestors in the jungle to survive against the forces of nature – against predators and all sorts of wild obstacles.

So we built communities, but it's not enough to build communities. The members in that community must have a neurological bond with that community – they must have a craving to belong to that community. You cannot just gather some people and say, this is my community. They must feel that they are part of that community in order for the community to survive against all odds, which at that time, that is, in the kingdom of the wild was rather imperative.

So being in a community means we are psychologically wired to feel that we are part of that community, which brings along an innate craving to be accepted by others in that community – by the majority of that community – to look for approval in everything that we do from fellow members of that community – to look for appreciation for our actions – to look for appraisal from others, for our achievements, for our successes.

In the wild, it worked well. And even today it keeps a people together. That's okay. So it is not completely harmful, but what is harmful is that this very trait has also a negative side and rather devastatingly negative side, which is that this craving, this social conditioning often compels a person to go against their own passion, their own uniqueness to be accepted by the society. So the person ends up doing what the society wants instead of doing what that person really wanted to do in the first place, whether it is about living life, whether it is about achieving a certain goal, or anything else.

In the end, the majority of people end up achieving the goals that the society wishes them to achieve as members of the community. And the same goes for wishes, the same goes for desires, the same goes for behaviors, the same goes for thought, the same goes for emotions and feelings and sentiments and ambitions and so on. So we ended up living secondhand lives. We end up living lives of mindless machines – we end up living lives of slaves of the society instead of living the life that we want.

If a person is happy with living the way that the person is living while following the norms of the society, then that's completely fine. But if the person has to completely change himself or herself to follow the norms of the society, then that's dangerous and downright inhuman because all the progress that we have attained so far as a species took place because of the handful of so-called misfits who had the courage to go against the societal norms, to follow their dreams, to follow their passions, to follow their own original thoughts and ideas and inklings.

In short, rules and regulations of a society do not ensure progress. In fact, the rules that the society creates are there to ensure security, not to ensure progress. To ensure progress, one must first sacrifice security – only then can one achieve something that nobody has achieved ever before – one must have the guts to turn a blind eye to the mockery, the criticisms, the disapprovals of one's society. Only by doing this can one achieve what the person really wants for himself or herself.

This doesn't mean rebelling against society violently or aggressively – it simply means paying no attention to the society's selfish expectations, instead, the person must focus all their attention, all their energy on the one idea that is most important to them – to that one dream, that one passion, that one purpose, which defines who they are.

Life is not fully lived, until you are willing to die for your dream. Everybody dreams, but only few persist on their dream. Infinite patience, infinite purity and infinite perseverance are the key to achieving your dream.

What is a dream? A dream is an imagination, which can only become reality if accompanied by persistent actions, regardless of incessant failures. Failures bring clarity. Imagine someone's holding your head under water and you are struggling for air - such should be the yearning for a dream. One who has such yearning, can't be thwarted even with a thousand failures. So, it all comes down to one simple question - what is your yearning? What are you mad about? What are you crazy about? What is it that's more important to you than your life?

Your life is your decision – your life is your design – your life is your creation. One who realizes this, needs not rely on illusive saviors and deities. The world needs heroes. Be a hero and build your part of the world. Never mind the mistakes. One day they will become your most prized possessions.

Remember, you don't die when your body stops functioning. You die when your name is uttered for the last time in the world. So, stop grovelling and start working. Throw away the newspapers. Discard all the useless debates and gossiping. Start working in silence. Start working on your passion – on your dream – on your vision. And make the news yourself.

Don't just build a career, build a legacy. And don't let the illusion of destiny keep you from doing what you love to do - for nothing is meant to be, or not to be - it is only your willful and persistent action that determines your destiny.

Be possessed, not with the evils of selfishness and bigotry, but with the values and vigor of humanhood. Be possessed with courage. Be possessed with conscience. Be possessed with the power of reasoning. And above all, be possessed with tremendous confidence in the self.

If you say, "let there be light", and then act with all your capacity to make it a reality, only then there will be light and hope in the world. And forget not, in order to attain extraordinary greatness, first you need to be drowned in the deepest fathoms of helplessness, misery and heartache. So, think of strength, dream of strength, live of strength.

Let me tell you a story. There was a pond right next to the house I grew up in. One afternoon while playing by the pond, I accidentally fell in it. There was nobody around at that time as it was afternoon and everybody was sleeping, and I was yet to learn swimming. So, I prayed to all the gods and goddesses like all the adult kids did in that culture. But no god or deity came to my rescue. So, I struggled under the murky water and finally managed to survive by pulling myself to the bank. Perhaps that was the first sign I received from Nature about the true helplessness of life. While you are drowning, no god is going to come to your rescue, so learn to swim my friend, because it is only you, the living god on earth, who can save yourself and nobody else. The only god there is, is your will to live - so, be aware of that Himalayan will and make it as conscientious as possible, for then only, can your godliness have any impact upon your life as well as the lives of others.

Nobody wants great things for you. They all want you to be something they deem important for them. When the mind is infested with more judgement, conclusions and biases, than the actual urge for understanding, even the sun appears to be a candle and the ocean a pool. So, when everyone hails you insane especially because of your dream, remember this, all great achievements of humanity begin with the madness of a few lion-hearts. And the only quality that distinguishes the greats from the masses, is the unwillingness to give up.

Birth of Civilization

There is nothing special in existing - all animals do that. An existence can be called life only if it serves a purpose - a purpose that not simply benefits the self, but more importantly the society. The difference between survival and life is purpose. The difference between animal and human is purpose. In purpose you'll find courage - in purpose you'll find clarity - in purpose you'll find resilience - and above all, in purpose you'll find yourself.

Be immersed in your purpose - be immersed in your dream - become the embodiment of your dream - of your purpose - like, say, I am an embodiment of a united humanity. Uniting humanity is not just my dream or purpose, it is the very life-blood that runs through my veins - I and my dream are one - I and my purpose are one. Hence, Naskar is not a name, it is an insignia of a united humanity.

Each human must become the insignia of their dream, only then will there be hope for a brave, liberated and enlightened society. Right now we are doing quite the opposite, as depicted in the last chapter. We are creepy crawlers and we are raising creepy crawlers, instead of raising heroes. This must change - not tomorrow, but today. We must become heroes and we must raise heroes.

If there is one gospel that I could give you - it's this - be gods and make gods. Be what you want your society to be. If you want a patriotic world where people care for others as much as they care for themselves, be the person who cares for others as much for the self. Be patriotic and slowly but surely the world will become patriotic - be humane and slowly but surely the world will become humane - be human and slowly but surely the world will become human. It all starts with one person - it all starts with you.

Patriotism starts and ends with the individual - peace starts and ends with the individual - harmony starts and ends with the individual - the entire human civilization starts and ends with the individual - with you. So it doesn't matter whether a hundred people in a community are patriotic or not, what matters is whether that community has at least one individual bold and awake enough to take the all the responsibility of that community on his or her shoulder.

And no matter how absurd or impractical the vision of the individual may sound, without these absurd visions of individuals from various corners of the world, our entire human civilization will first come to a standstill and then fall back into the pit of primitiveness.

Practical and impractical are all human constructs. What a hundred people find impractical, may be practical to one person and if that one person gives all their life to that one impractical idea, it'll become the most practical ingredient of human progress.

Intellectuals and celebrities may cry, peace, peace – harmony, harmony – progress, progress, but no peace, progress and harmony can manifest outside the pages of books, unless the individual stands tall with the head held high and utters with utmost grace and glory to others - give me your agony and I will give you my life.

Recall the Declaration of Justice.

"In the course of human events, if ever, injustice grabs hold of the landscape that we the people

step foot on, it will be our organically divine right to abolish such injustice, with our thoughts, words and actions conscientious. We the people, each one of us, will do our utmost to create a society that needs not the intervention of law or any specialist authority. We will create a society of humans with our own two hands for the humans that are yet to be born, so that they may know justice and order in their life, which we have been deprived of due to the indifference and callousness of our ancestors. We the living, breathing and thinking humans do solemnly declare upon our functional conscience, that from this moment onwards, we will no longer adhere to the traditional habit of dependency, hypocrisy and meekness, and we will come to the aid of every human who faces injustice in any form, with this golden principle engraved upon our hearts, that there are no foreigners, only family."

- **Operation Justice: To Make A Society That Needs No Law**

Say out loud - I am in humanity - humanity is in me - from me starts civilization - in me ends civilization. I and the species are not separate, but one. I am the species, the species is me. I am the society, the society is me - such should be the fundamental thinking of a patriot, and indeed of a human, for patriot and human are one and the same - a human without responsibility towards the society is an animal - and the responsibility towards one's society is true patriotism. Hence, either one is a patriot or an animal, it is this simple.

Raising Heroes with Education

Unfortunate and uncivilized though it may sound, in many parts of the human society, nay, most parts of the human society, one's worth is measured by the amount of money one earns, not by the value one adds to the society. And this has become the greatest curse of humankind – the greatest impediment to our global progress. If Mandela, King, Teresa, Bose (the man behind India's Independence, not the Physicist) and other legends of human history ran like dogs chasing money, instead of thinking of their society, we wouldn't have a civilized and free world to live in.

But the point is, we still don't have a truly civilized and free society around the world. The whole world still needs the sacrifice of countless more legends, but the problem is, these legends face nothing but obstruction from their own society. Nevertheless, without the sacrifice of many more heroes in our time, this world can never become the true abode of peace, harmony and progress for the generations to come. The sun is known by its light, the tree is known by its fruits, the human is known by its sacrifice.

And, the people who can't sacrifice anything, must, at the very least, stop being egotistical and know-it-all snobs, and give a hand to those individuals who are trying to make a difference. And if they can't help in any manner, at least, they must try not to discourage the budding champions of progress. It's hard as it is for the torchbearers, so if you can't support them, do not criticize them. Criticism is the weapon of the lesser human – it's the weapon of the creature that's incapable of original thinking and original action.

I'm pain stricken to say that even many of the parents around the world feed fear into the heart of their children as they grow up, and then they expect great things from them. They train their children from an early age to compete with their friends, to see their friends as enemies, to focus on earning instead of learning, they breed and raise race-horses, and then they foolishly dream of a beautiful, progressive and humane society for those children.

A person with a broken leg can walk by the help of prosthetic, but no prosthetic can fix a broken spirit. Day after day the so-called modern society keeps killing the spirit of champions –

they keep killing the hearts that hold the force for greatness and progress. Yet these people who murder the spirit of greatness on a daily basis, are never held accountable for their actions. In fact, they take pride in such actions, and they call it either sensibility or responsibility. It's not responsibility my friend, nor is it sensibility, it's irresponsibility and primitiveness at their worst.

People take pride in their historical heroes, but when a hero is born in their own family, they'd do everything in their power to trample his or her spirit. They look up to the achievements of the world's legends, but they can't manage to comprehend that most of those achievements were not born of conventional thinking. They survive more on fear than water and oxygen. They eat fear, dream fear, live fear and then they pass on that fear to their children. Naturally, each day the world keeps losing a dream, each day the world keeps losing a champion.

To the parents I say, if you can't afford to give your child the right to pursue their dreams, you have no right to breed. However, if you genuinely want to be responsible parents, then learn to be selfless in raising your kids. And by selfless, I don't mean that fake selflessness, where you believe that you are being selfless, but in reality you keep imposing all your desires and dreams on your kids. Be genuinely selfless and give your kids the courage to go after their dreams. And whatever you do, don't program them to be afraid of failures, because without failure there's no learning, without failure there's no discovery, without failure there's no progress.

No school teaches a person to recognize and pursue their dreams, nor do they teach them to be a crutch to the society, they only manufacture selfish, egotistical, materialist snobs who live their whole life as slaves with the delusion of grandeur. Ask a child "what do you want to be when you grow up", they would say "I want to become a doctor and save lives - I want to become a cop and protect the innocent - I want to become a soldier and defend my people." But ask the same question after they finish their education, and their answer would be "I want to get a highly paid job - I want to buy a large mansion - I want to be a millionaire". Here I ask you, who turned a hero into a selfish, insecure narcissist? It's our system of education.

The ragged system of education that we have today was designed in the ancient times to manufacture mechanical slaves. And today, all our children's hopes and dreams turn to ashes in exam papers - their delicate baby wings crack under the weight of books - the classroom ends up as prison and to dream becomes a criminal offence. This is not education, this is bestiality.

And despite all our progress, most of which have been pioneered by misfits outside the conventional education structure, we still keep on using such primitive system. The system of education since the moment of its birth has remained more or less the same, despite the revolutionary changes across the world. And in many cases, people actually take pride in the lifelessness of such system. The most striking example that appears in my mind right now, is the pride of the Indian population on an abundance of Indian origin CEOs in the world.

Apparently, right now, some of the most important companies in the world are run by India-born CEOs. And this looks rather lucrative to the Indians all over world, because it makes them feel a sense of superiority. But the fact of the matter is, none of those companies were founded by any India-born person.

The system of education in India as well as all over the world is good at producing laborers, that's all. And since India is about to be the largest population on earth, it's no surprise that many of the highly professional and more importantly mechanical CEOs of the world would end up Indian or India-born. And, while Indian CEOs in Non-Indian companies are getting all the praise and admiration from the Indians, startups born on Indian soil remain unrecognized - this is not a matter of pride, it's a matter of shame, especially for a population whose history is replete with mathematical, scientific and philosophical achievements.

Mind-expanding education is what the world needs. If an education doesn't nourish and expand the capacities of the mind then what is the point of such education! Throw away such education that teaches a child to be selfish - throw away such education that teaches a child to forget their passion - throw away such education that teaches a child to be like everybody else - throw away such education that produces second hand humans instead of raising original, conscientious beings of character.

And we must start by shifting the focus of education from personal gain to collective growth. Once we have done that, that is, once we are clear on our vision of our collective growth, then comes the development of a less mechanical and more organic model of education. Now comes the most important question - what would an organic model of education be like?

In an organic model of education, the purpose of teaching should be to give students the tools to recognize their own unique interest without feeling judged, and once they've recognized it, to prepare them to be excellent at it. In short, the purpose of education should be to nourish and strengthen a student's capacity, not to force-feed all students the same material, till they either pass some baseless test, or drop out of education altogether, - or commit suicide.

If a student commits suicide because they couldn't bear the pressure of education, it's not a sign of their weakness, but that of the system of education. To prevent that, the society must recognize that weakness. And so far, the situation has been far from it. The society has remained in denial towards the destructive aspects of its education system since its birth. And that's the reason, why most of humankind's greatest achievements, if not all, have come from individuals outside the education system. Or to put it more blatantly - progress is caused by the rejects of the education system.

So, the question is, what kind of education is it that has no capacity to recognize potential! It's not education, it's a catastrophe. And it's time that we deal with this catastrophe head on. We cannot educate the citizens of tomorrow based on the requirements of yesterday. But mark you, this doesn't mean a collision between two systems, rather it simply means an evolution from the primitive and mechanical system into an organic and civilized system.

And if you are wondering how this evolution can take place - it's this simple - forget about the grand system of education as a whole and just pay attention to the education of any one school you are involved with, either as a parent or a teacher or in any other capacity. Start discussing with other parents, teachers, other school authorities and local psychologists, on how you can develop a more creative, organic and whole education model for your school alone, and once you have a rough idea of the model, implement it and collectively keep record of the over-all wellbeing of the children, not just their academic performance. And over time, do the necessary moderations to the system, based on the gathered data. And when your school begins to raise healthy and whole human beings instead of raising robots, other schools will automatically follow in your footsteps. Change of an entire education system begins with change in the pedagogy of one school. Turn one school from a robot factory into a cradle of heroes, and the very face of education on earth will change.

Mainspring of Life

Mainspring of Life (A Sonnet)

From "The Constitution of The United Peoples of Earth"

I have no nationality except humanity,
I have no tradition except compassion,
I have no religion except liberty,
I have no god except a family of 7 billion,
I have no belief but only awareness,
I have no creed but only acceptance,
I have no messiah except the self,
I have no scripture except my conscience,
I have no gospel except godliness,
I have no sermon except thought,
I have no philosophy except oneness,
I have nothing to give you except love a whole
lot,
I demand no obedience, nor do I desire worship
and offering,
For there is death in worship, and freedom is
life's mainspring.

Earning The Title of Human

My body is a temple and each cell in it holds the image of my God - my humankind. Whatever I do I do for my God - whatever I create I create to serve my God - whatever I discover I discover to aid my God. My work is my offering to my God - my life is my offering to my God, for I have nothing grander to offer than my life. So, behold my humanity, thou shalt always find me standing next to you, during your darkest days and fiercest nights – thou shalt never be alone, so long as thou have faith in me, nay yourself - for I and you are not separate - I live nowhere else but in you - you live nowhere else but in me. Look deeply, look beyond and thou shall be free.

You are your own freedom - you are your own peace - you are your own salvation. Seek these traits, virtues and states nowhere else but within the deepest fathoms of yourself. Seek your powers - seek your capacities within you - then bring them out into the world to serve the society, for service of society - service of the collective, is the highest utilization of the force of life. This service is the very seed of everything that we hold civilized and pure, for selfishness is death, service is life. And this very service is the lifeforce of patriotism.

Patriotism doesn't mean blind mindless allegiance to any national, political or religious identity, patriotism means offering oneself in the service of others in one's society. Here the society is simply the representation of a collective of people - that collective could be a neighborhood - it could be a city - state – county - or it could also be an entire planet. Here it's the people that count, not their superficial identities - it's the lives that count, not the labels placed on them for the purpose of identification. It is this simple. Service of others is patriotism - service of others is holiness - service of others is humanity. In short, patriotism is holiness, holiness is humanity.

There is no place for hatred and discrimination in patriotism, either against the people from other nations, or from any background different from one's own. In fact, in patriotism there is no place for sectarian superficial identities, such as that of nation, religion or any other. In real patriotism, all superficial identities vanish and what remains is an incorruptible sense of union with the people around. In the nameless space of mind, the space between minds vanishes.

It's time we take the leap across the infectious carcass of nationalism and rise as patriots of humanity - as patriots of a planet (until we come across intelligent lifeforms in other planets) and not of any nation, religion or language. And you can take that leap, only if you have an indomitable sense of oneness with all of humankind. From this oneness rises the purest force of patriotism - the force, called love.

Love is the bridge between you and everyone else. Fortified with the force of love only can we build a truly united world. Some skeptics may question, why do we need to build a united world at all! And my answer to them is, a united world is a humane world, whereas a divided world is a savage world. Division or segregation of any kind breeds disharmony - to have harmony, we must erase all segregation.

True meaning of patriotism is not discrimination and segregation, it is equality and inclusion. And so long as the forces of equality and inclusion run through the veins of even ten patriots, no brainless bigot can succeed in poisoning the soul of our beautiful and graceful planet. Whatever happens to our planet, good or bad, it's on us - on each one of us - each human being, because no extraterrestrial savior is coming down to liberate our planet from the shackles of atrocities caused by the so-called intelligent humans.

Jesus is long gone, he is not coming back. Worshipping him and hoping for his so-called second coming may give you comfort, but it doesn't do anything for either Jesus or the society. The only way you can make any difference in the lives of others as well as your own, is by becoming Christ-like in character and action. In fact, being a christian is not about being Christ-fearing, it's about being Christ-like.

Reincarnation is an ancient myth, nothing more - it is the fairytale of the adults. And as long as it alleviates people's anxiety, it is an acceptable myth, but the moment it becomes an impediment to life, it turns deadly for the individual as well as the society. The history of human civilization on earth is filled with such myths, and there is nothing wrong in accepting them as part of our life, as long we take them as what they are, that is, myths, but if we take them to be facts and begin to ignore actual facts, then such behavior only breeds more prejudice, bigotry and discrimination.

No messiah is coming to save us or our world, it is us who have to save ourselves as well as our world. We are our own responsibility - our world is our responsibility - our people are our responsibility. And anybody who takes the responsibility of their society on their shoulder, is a patriot - such a person is the real Christ, real Buddha, real Naskar of their time.

Jesus died about two thousand years ago - Buddha died about five hundred years before that - and so will I. But our ideas of liberty, conscience and character will never perish from the face of this earth, so long as there is even one human being awake enough to see the society as their own family. So long as there is even one person whose lifeblood is liberty, I will never die, nor will Buddha, Jesus, King, Teresa and all other patriots of humanity.

Rise O Brave being of thunder and be an Atlas - rise as the Titan whose sole mission in life is to care for others - to be the crutch to the broken souls - to be the answer to the prayers of countless innocent lives stuck in misery. Never ask what the world has given you, ask what you can give the world, for you are the key to the world's misery. The world is sick and you are its cure. In you is the light, in you is the might, come riding your fiery steed and light up even the darkest night. Keep your head high and be a shining emblem of courage for those who are too afraid to raise their head. Be the spark of dignity for them - be the spark of serenity for them - be the spark of sanity for them - be the spark of sanctity for them.

You are not immortal and you don't have to be - you are a mortal - a mortal being of flesh and blood, who will perish one day, just like every other living creature. But if you use your life to improve the lives of even five people, that will be the highest fulfillment of your life, no matter how long you live. Life lived for others is human life, whereas life lived for only the self is animal life. So, choose today, what do you want to die as, a human being or an animal? All humans are born as animals, it's only by our actions that we must earn the title of human – the title of sapiens.

Sonnet of Sapiens

Sonnet of Sapiens

From "Fabric of Humanity"

No religion is greater than love,
For love is the embodiment of divinity,
No church is higher than the self,
Cause the self is the manifestation of the
Almighty,
No worship is greater than help,
For helping is the service of God,
No prayer is as sacred as kindness,
For in kindness lies the real act of the Lord,
No scripture is more glorious than the mind,
For the mind is the creator of the scriptures,
So learn from that scripture within to be of help
to your kind,
And be the glue to the fabric of humanity
healing all ruptures,
Heal your kind my friend with your wisdom
and warmth transcendent,
If not you then who else will unify humanity
and rise as sapiens triumphant.

Lives to Serve Before I Sleep

Lives to Serve Before I Sleep
From "Lives To Serve Before I Sleep"

Lives to serve before I sleep,
Cause service is my salvation;
Wounds to heal before I sleep,
Cause time is wailing for absolution;
Bridges to build before I sleep,
Cause too many walls are raised already;
Peoples to unite before I sleep,
Cause civilization is trembling and walking
unsteady.

Shackles to shatter before I sleep,
Cause corruption festers in the stagnant norm;
Labels to erase before I sleep,
Cause they've only confused our global dorm;
Sects to humanize before I sleep,
Cause segregation has weakened the human
bond;
Blades to burn before I sleep,
Cause they've turned the world into a bloody
pond.

Tears to wipe before I sleep,
Cause the society is lost in fun;
Homes to heal before I sleep,
Cause ego has wrecked the nests a ton;
Biases to alleviate before I sleep,
Cause bigotry has outweighed compassion;
Purity to pour before I sleep,
Cause all are chasing petty gratification.

Spirits to lift before I sleep,
Cause the minds are running dry;
Gods to build before I sleep,
Cause orthodoxy makes humanity cry;
Wars to end before I sleep,
Cause no life is expendable and puny;
Humans to raise before I sleep,
Cause where humans act human there reigns
harmony.

If No One Comes, Walk Alone

If No One Comes, Walk Alone (A Sonnet)

If no one comes hearing your call - walk alone,
For the price of rigidity is greater than the cost
of a fall.
If no one comes hearing your call - speak alone,
For the price of silence is greater than the cost of
a scorn.
If no one comes hearing your call - reason alone,
For the price of prejudice is greater than the cost
of loneliness.
If no one comes hearing your call - think alone,
For the price of bigotry is greater than the cost of
feeling groundless.
If no one comes hearing your call - dream alone,
For the price of conformity is greater than the
cost of failure.
If no one comes hearing your call - act alone,
For the price of inaction is greater than the cost
of alleged misdemeanor.
If no one comes hearing your call, o brave titan -
carry the society on your own,
For peace, progress and harmony are caused by
the acts of the one alone.

Being Patriot is Being Human

What happens to our world is personal to all of us and it must be taken as such, for if you think that the problems of this world are none of your business or that they don't affect you directly, then you couldn't be more foolishly deluded. While it is true that many of the problems of our world may not affect us directly and instantly, but they unavoidably will have direct implications in the life our children and grandchildren.

Being a patriot and being a human are not different - in their purest form they are one and the same. We only look at them differently because our society has conditioned us to look at the outside appearance of things. Naturally, most people can perceive the obvious outside appearance of things, but to go deeper, piercing the surface of appearance, is the real skill of a sage. So, let's go deep, shall we - you and me together, not as some pompous self-proclaimed sage, but simply as plain, ordinary, curious and rather naïve children.

The separation among these terms is completely illusive, born of our socially induced conventional tenet to use them in different contexts. And the more you use a certain word in a certain context and hear a certain word being used in a certain context, over time your brain builds up a neural mesh of psychological correlation between the word and the context you use it in. This is called classical conditioning. Let me elaborate with an example of utter significance in our present world. Take the word Islam. A huge portion of the human population has been conditioned to elicit an instinctual fear response whenever they hear the term "Islam" or related term. This is what we call Islamophobia. It is not merely a matter of social stigma - it has much deeper biological roots. And the only way to uproot this societal vice is to destroy its biological roots, not by force, but with the force of wisdom. For this purpose we must understand the biological bases of this specific socially conditioned phobia.

In this context I must mention the name of the person whose experiment discovered the phenomenon of classical conditioning. And the person was the Russian physiologist Ivan Petrovich Pavlov. He discovered the concept of conditional reflex while examining the rates of salivations among dogs.

Pavlov was fascinated to notice that when a bell (conditioned stimulus) was rang followed by presentation of food (unconditioned stimulus) to a dog in consecutive sequences, it would initially salivate when the food was presented. But eventually, the dog would come to associate the sound with the presentation of the food and salivate immediately upon the presentation of that conditioned stimulus of sound, even without the presentation of the unconditioned stimulus of food.

So, to put it simply, in classical conditioning, an animal learns to respond to a neutral stimulus in the same way it would respond to an effective stimulus. And Islamophobia is the product of such a conditioning. At a cellular level of the human mind, it is a natural biological fear response of the general social psyche, conditioned through countless pairings between terrorist attacks (unconditioned stimulus) and their apparent association with Islam (conditioned stimulus). Hence, Islamophobia cannot be eradicated completely simply by force, talks and debates, unless that pairing is severed and thereafter the conditioned stimulus of Islam is paired with something optimistic such as the heartwarming works of the 13th century Persian Muslim poet Jalal ad-Din Muhammad Rumi.

The point is, till this day, in usual circumstances of daily human life, the truth holds very little bearing over people's personal psychological perception of the word. It is all personal, and has nothing to do with reality. It's about belief and not the truth - it's about feeling and not thought. When enough people possess the same belief, that belief automatically turns into an irrefutable truth in the eyes of the people, even if that belief happens to be the most atrocious lie of all times.

The society till this day runs hugely on belief and not on the foundation of truth. This belief is based primarily on feelings and very little on facts. And when it comes to facts, people don't care about facts, unless they can feel those facts in their bones. So, to make facts accepted and embraced by the general population, it is not enough to present them as mere packets of data or raw information - they must be presented soaked in feelings. Let's conduct a brief thought experiment to elaborate this matter. For this purpose I am using climate change as an example. I'll present to you two statements, saying basically the same thing.

Statement 1: The average temperature of the earth has increased exponentially in the recent times, which has begun to cause never before seen extreme weather events. These extreme weather events are placing human lives across the world at great risk. And the only way to reduce these events is to reduce green-house gas emission. You as an individual can do it by driving less, consuming electricity less and plating trees more.

Statement 2: Imagine your kids burning or drowning to death. It hurts, doesn't it! That's exactly the kind of future that awaits your kids, unless you step up. Stop being the nonchalant speculator and act responsible. What can you do, you ask! Here's what you can do right now. Drive less, consume electricity less and plant trees more.

Now, here simply contemplate on which of these two statements holds more significance to you - hopefully it's the second one. That's because, while in the first statement, the truth is presented raw, without any additives, in the second statement the truth is on purpose dipped in the linguistic potion of feelings. And Mother Nature's selective pressure on our brain has conditioned us to be vulnerable to feelings, not to facts, or even truth for that matter.

We feel first and think later. In fact, some of the greatest achievements of humankind have been sparked by feelings - by emotions. Even my so-called works of science and philosophy have been triggered by emotions. I say so-called because the more I write, the more I find it hard to describe my work with any contemporary label. Science has its limitations, so does philosophy, as well as every single feat of the human mind. And the purpose of my work is to point out those limitations as well as the responsibility of each field in the human society, in the gentlest and most naïve manner possible, with the purpose of building a united humanity.

I have a dream - that one day, black people won't be black - white people won't be white - brown people won't be brown - gay people won't be gay - straight people won't be straight - women won't be women - men won't be men -

the trans won't be trans - believers won't be believers and non-believers won't be non-believers - instead, we all will be just human. And once we are all just human, the very need for terms like "patriot", "humanitarian", "social responsibility", "social service" will fade away.

Some people believe, the destiny of humans is written by God, and I know for a fact, that human destiny is written by none but the humans. And I don't give a damn whether I am right or not, but whenever I see someone in trouble, I do not wait for some illusive benevolent Father or Mother to intervene. The greatest use of life is to ease the trouble of others. I am a plain ordinary human in the service of the humans - service is my oxygen, service is my water, service is my bread and service is my butter. I exist to serve and I'll die serving.

There is no greater happiness than in relieving the sorrow of others. There is no greater joy, than being an ingredient in the joy of others. There is no greater patriotism than this - there is no greater humanism than this - there is no greater religion than this - there is no higher divinity than this.

Divinity is humanity - humanity is kindness - but it's not some superficial kindness, pompously called "charity" - it's kindness without expectation. Kindness with expectation is no kindness. Goodness is only goodness when practiced without expectation. When you feel selfish enough to lose yourself in helping others, that's when a patriot is born - that's when an animal turns into a human.

Without patriotism, that is, a sense of responsibility towards the society, a creature is not human to begin with. So, think again. What are you! Do not answer me. Just think. And if the very question offends or bothers you in any way, then you should rethink why you are reading me in the first place. There are certain questions which I can answer with facts - but the most important questions of life do not have any factual answers. Each individual must work out their own answers to these questions. And mark you, no one - and I mean no one can spoon-feed you the answers, no matter how much some know-it-all charlatans shout otherwise.

We always look for solutions outside, without realizing that they lie within us. And when people are foolish enough to seek solutions from others, which they are already in possession of, it's only natural that charlatans queue across the world to cash in on that foolishness. Here, I am not talking about the experts of various fields, such as scientists, doctors, philosophers and others - I am talking about those apes who are commonly worshiped by fools as mystics, yogis and gurus.

There is nothing wrong in following a teacher in the path of self-awareness, but the moment one begins to see that teacher as the authority of one's life, immediately one goes astray from the path of self-realization and indeed from the path of truth, and eventually ends up in the same kind of trap of doctrines and laws that one wanted to be free from in the first place. That's how all religions have been born.

Loyalty to a teacher or messiah, inadvertently leads to psychological slavery, and in often cases, the enslaved is not even aware of the enslavement. It's a kind of illusion one lives in, where the teacher's words or the prophet's doctrines become gospel in the life of an individual. Hence, all shortcomings of that teacher or prophet creep into the life of his followers as well.

The first step to self-realization is the realization of the fact that no one can give you freedom - no one can give you the answers to the most complex questions of your life. You have to figure them out yourself. Nobody has it all figured out, not even me - anybody who thinks otherwise, is an idiot. I can tell you the biological roots of your desires and drives, but implementing that factual information in a practical manner in your life is completely on you.

The only sin in this world is to lose faith in yourself. Belief in God, messiah or some spiritual con-artist is optional, but belief in the self is imperative. Be your own guru. Learn to be true to yourself, and everything good will follow. Turn your thoughts within and become a sage yourself. Don't be a disciple to anybody. Let you own mind be your guru. Become the pupil of your own conscience.

Let the lotus of your character be full-blown and the results will follow. Awaken your mind from the deep sleep of ancient mysticism and make it self-conscious - power will come, glory will come, goodness will come and everything that is excellent will come.

Be brave and upright. Shred the fake mask of humility into pieces. And put on the mask of arrogance if needed. Take the whole responsibility of your neighborhood, of your people, of your society on your own shoulders. If not a big banyan tree, at least be like a mango tree under the shade of which a few people can rest. You are the architect of this beautiful planet. Build it your way. And nourish it with your actual civilized conscience.

"Do something so radical that the laws of nature are shaken,
Do something so radical that your very existence becomes someone's dream,
Do something so radical that it appears impossible to your brethren,
Do something so radical that others either hate you or worship you to the extreme,
Do something so radical that your breath becomes someone's mental essence,
Do something so radical that the intellectuals keep silent in front of you,
Do something so radical that the weak regains strength by your presence,
Do something so radical that no one can ever repay with all the I O U,

*Do something so radical that no death can ever
make you perish,
Do something so radical that all the sons and
prophets pay you heed,
Do something so radical that your immortality
makes history cherish,
Do something so radical that the meekest of
slaves starts to lead,
Do something my friend that matters to
humanity beyond the society's wildest
imagination,
Thus you get to be the solution and not the
problem like the rest of the population."*

- ## Build Bridges Not Walls: In The Name of Americana

Mind not the pain, for one who knows pain, can help others without gain. Don't be frightened by your wounds, celebrate them as priceless relics born of your toil. The more the scars, the greater your impact on the world. Mind you, life is not measured in years, it's measured in actions. Act with all your might and conscience, for it's only with our actions that we are remembered after we fall asleep. Your identity lies not in your name or your background, but in your actions. Action is life, inaction is death.

Come out of your den o lions and lionesses of the world and roar to awaken everyone. Mind not your scars, for your scars will leave a sacred trail which will bear testimony to your voyage. Awake and arise from the torturous confinement of your insecurities with fiery wings and rock the world, only to settle the foundation stones of true humanity.

BIBLIOGRAPHY

Archer M., (2000), Being Human: The Problem of Agency. Cambridge University Press.

Archer M., (2003), Structure, Agency and the Internal Conversation. Cambridge University Press.

Adolphs R (2003) Cognitive neuroscience of human social behaviour. Nature Rev Neurosci 4: 165–178.

Adolphs R, Tranel D, Damasio AR (2003) Dissociable neural systems for recognizing emotions. Brain Cogn 52: 61–69.

Afton, A. D. (1985). Forced copulation as a reproductive strategy of male lesser scaup: A field test of some predictions. - Behaviour 92, p. 146-167.

Allison T, Puce A, McCarthy G. (2000) Social perception from visual cues: role of the STS region. Trends Cogn Sci 4: 267–278.

Andresen, Jensine, and Robert Forman, eds. Cognitive Models and Spiritual Maps. Bowling Green, Ohio: Imprint Academic, 2000.

Ashbrook, James, and Carol Albright. The Humanizing Brain: Where Religion and Neuroscience Meet. Cleveland, OH: Pilgrim Press, 1997.

Azari, Nina, Janpeter Nickel, Gilbert Wunderlich, Michael Niedeggen, Harald Hefter, Lutz Tellmann, Hans Herzog, Petra Stoerig, Dieter Birnbacher, and Rudiger Seitz. "Neural Correlates of Religious Experience." European Journal of Neuroscience 13, no. 8 (2001)

Agar, N. (2004). Liberal eugenics: In defence of human enhancement. London: Blackwell Publishing.

Alteheld, N., Roessler, G., Vobig, M., & Walter, R. (2004). The retina implant new approach to a visual prosthesis. Biomedizinische Technik, 49(4), 99–103.

Antal, A., Nitsche, M. A., Kincses, T. Z., Kruse, W., Hoffmann, K. P., & Paulus, W. (2004a). Facilitation of visuo-motor learning by transcranial direct current stimulation of the motor and extrastriate visual areas in humans. European Journal of Neuroscience, 19(10), 2888–2892.

Bhat Z, Kumar, S, Bhat H (2015) In vitro meat production. Challenges and benefits over conventional meat production. J Sci Food Agric 14: 241–248

Bernstein R. J., (1967), John Dewey. New York: Washington Square Press.

Bernstein R.J., (1971), Praxis and Action: Contemporary Philosophies of Human Activity. Philadelphia: University of Pennsylvania Press.

Bernstein R.J., (1976), The Restructuring Social and Political Thought.

Bernstein R.J., (1983), Beyond Relativism and Objectivism: Science, Hermeneutics, and Praxis. Philadelphia: University of Pennsylvania Press.

Bernstein R.J., (1986), Philosophical Profiles. Philadelphia: University of Pennsylvania Press.

Bernstein R.J., (1991), New Constellation. Cambridge: MIT Press.

Barash, D. P. (1977). Sociobiology of rape in mallards (Anas platyrhynchos): Responses of the mated male. - Science 197, p. 788-789.

Berger, J. (1986). Wild horses of the great basin: Social competition and population size. - The University of Chicago Press, Chicago.

Birkhead, T. R., Johnson, S. D. & Nettleship, D. N. (1985). Extra-pair matings and mate guarding in the common murre Uria aalge. - Anim. Behav. 33, p. 608-619.

Beauregard, Mario, and Vincent Paquette. "Neural Correlates of a Mystical Experience in Carmelite Nuns." Neuroscience Letters 405, no. 3 (2006)

Benson, Herbert. Timeless Healing: The Power and Biology of Belief. New York: Scribner, 1996

Bogen, J.E.(1995a), 'On the neurophysiology of consciousness: Part I. An overview', Consciousness and Cognition, 4.

Bogen, J.E. (1995b), 'On the neurophysiology of consciousness: Part II. Constraining the semantic problem', Consciousness and Cognition, 4.

Bremner, J. D., R. Soufer, et al. (2001). "Gender differences in cognitive and neural correlates of remembrance of emotional words." Psychopharmacol Bull 35 (3).

Brothers, L. (2002). The social brain: A project for integrating primate behavior and neurophysiology in a new domain. In J. T. Cacioppo et al. (Eds.), Foundations in neuroscience. Cambridge, MA: MIT Press.

Buss, D. D. (2003). Evolutionary Psychology: The New Science of Mind, 2nd ed. New York: Allyn & Bacon.

Buss, D. M. (1989). "Conflict between the sexes: Strategic interference and the evocation of anger and upset." J Pers Soc Psychol 56 (5).

Buss, D. M. (1995). "Psychological sex differences. Origins through sexual selection." Am Psychol 50 (3).

Buss, D. M. (2002). "Review: Human Mate Guarding." Neuro Endocrinol Lett 23 (Suppl 4).

Buss, D. M., and D. P. Schmitt (1993). "Sexual strategies theory: An evolutionary perspective on human mating." Psychol Rev 100 (2).

Blakemore SJ, Decety J (2001) From the perception of action to the understanding of intention. Nature Rev Neurosci 2: 561.

Bruce C, Desimone R, Gross CG (1981) Visual properties of neurons in a polysensory area in superior temporal sulcus of the macaque. J Neurophysiol 46: 369–384.

Buccino G, Vogt S, Ritzl A, Fink GR, Zilles K, Freund HJ, Rizzolatti G (2004) Neural circuits underlying imitation of hand actions: an event related fMRI study. Neuron 42: 323–34.

Colapietro V., (1988), "Human Agency: The Habits of Our Being."

Southern Journal of Philosophy, XXVI, 2, pp. 153-68.

Colapietro V., (1992), "Purpose, Power, and Agency." The Monist, 75, 4 (October) pp. 423-44.

Colapietro V., (2003), "Signs and their vicissitudes: Meanings in excess of consciousness and functionality." Logica, Dialogica, Ideologica, a cure di Susan Petrilli e Patrizia Calefato (Milano: Mimesis), pp. 221-36.

Colapietro V., (2004a), "C. S. Peirce's Reclamation of Teleology." Nature in American Philosophy, ed. Jean De Groot (Washington, D.C.: Catholic University Press of America), pp. 88-108.

Colapietro V., (2004b), "Portrait of a Historicist: An Alternative Reading of Peircean Semiotic." Semiotiche, 2/04 [maggio 2004], pp. 49-68.

Colapietro V., (2006), "Engaged Pluralism: Between Alterity and

Sociality." The Pragmatic Century: Conversations with Richard J. Bernstein (Albany, NY: SUNY Press), pp. 39-68.

Colapietro V., (2009), "Habit, Competence, and Purpose." Forthcoming in The Transactions of the Charles S. Peirce Society. Calder AJ, Keane J, Manes F, Antoun N, Young AW (2000) Impaired recognition and experience of disgust following brain injury. Nature Neurosci 3: 1077–1078.

Carey DP, Perrett DI, Oram MW (1997) Recognizing, understanding and reproducing actions. In: Jeannerod M, Grafman J (eds) Handbook of neuropsychology. Vol. 11: Action and cognition. Elsevier, Amsterdam.

Carr L, Iacoboni M, Dubeau MC, Mazziotta JC, Lenzi GL (2003) Neural mechanisms of empathy in humans: a relay from neural systems for imitation to limbic areas. Proc Natl Acad Sci USA 100: 5497–5502.

Changeux JP, Ricoeur P (1998) La nature et la règle. Odile Jacob, Paris.

Cochin S, Barthelemy C, Roux S, Martineau J (1999) Observation and execution of movement: similarities demonstrated by quantified electroencephalograpy. Eur J Neurosci 11: 1839– 1842.

Chomsky Noam, (2017) Requiem for the American Dream

Chomsky Noam, (2016) Who Rules the World?

Chomsky Noam, (2010) How the World Works

Churchland, P.S. (1986), Neurophilosophy (Cambridge, MA: The MIT Press).

Churchland, P.S. & Ramachandran, V.S. (1993), 'Filling in: Why Dennett is wrong', in Dennett and His Critics:

Demystifying Mind, ed. B. Dahlbom (Oxford: Blackwell Scientific Press).

Churchland, P.S., Ramachandran, V.S. & Sejnowski, T.J. (1994), 'A critique of pure vision', in Large- scale Neuronal Theories of the Brain, ed. C. Koch & J.L. Davis (Cambridge, MA: The MIT Press).

Crick, F. (1994), The Astonishing Hypothesis: The Scientific Search for the Soul (New York: Simon and Schuster).

Crick, F. (1996), 'Visual perception: rivalry and consciousness', Nature, 379.

Crick, F. & Koch, C. (1992), 'The problem of consciousness', Scientific American, 267.

Craig AD (2002) How do you feel? Interoception: the sense of the physiological condition of the body. Nature Rev Neurosci 3: 655–666.

Damasio, A (2003a) Looking for Spinoza. Harcourt Inc. Damasio A (2003b) Feeling of emotion and the self. Ann NY Acad Sci 1001: 253–261.

d'Aquili, Eugene. "Senses of Reality in Science and Religion." Zygon 17, no 4 (1982)

d'Aquili, Eugene. "The Biopsychological Determinants of Religious Ritual Behavior." Zygon 10, no. 1 (1975)

d'Aquili, Eugene. "The Myth-Ritual Complex: A Biogenetic Structural Analysis." Zygon 18, no. 3 (1983)

d'Aquili, Eugene, and Andrew Newberg. The Mystical Mind: Probing the Biology of Religious Experience. Minneapolis: Fortress Press, 1999.

Daly DD. 1958. Ictal affect. Am J Psychiatry.

Damasio, A. (1994) Descartes' Error: Emotion, Reason and the Human Brain. New York, Putnams.

Damasio, A. (1999) The Feeling of What Happens: Body, Emotion and the Making of Consciousness. London, Heinemann.

Darwin, C. (1859) On the Origin of Species by Means of Natural Selection. London, Murray.

Darwin, C. (1871) The Descent of Man and Selection in Relation to Sex. London, John Murray.

Darwin, C. (1872) The Expression of the Emotions in Man and Animals. London, John Murray; also published 1965, Chicago, University of Chicago Press.

Dawkins, M.S. (1987) Minding and mattering. In C. Blakemore and S. Greenfield (eds) Mindwaves. Oxford, Blackwell, 151-60.

Dawkins, R. (1976) The Selfish Gene. Oxford, Oxford University Press; a new edition, with additional material, was published in 1989.

Dawkins, R. (1986) The Blind Watchmaker. London, Longman.

Di Pellegrino G, Fadiga L, Fogassi L, Gallese V, Rizzolatti G (1992) Understanding motor events: A neurophysiological study. Exp Brain Res 91: 176–80.

Deikman, A.J. (2000) A functional approach to mysticism. Journal of Consciousness Studies 7(11-12), 75-91.

Delmonte, M.M. (1987) Personality and meditation. In M. West (ed.) The Psychology of Meditation. Oxford, Clarendon Press, 118-32.

Dennett, D.C. (1987) The Intentional Stance. Cambridge, MA, MIT Press.

Dennett, D.C. (1988) Quining qualia. In A.J. Marcel and E. Bisiach (eds)

Consciousness in Contemporary Science. Oxford, Oxford University Press, 42-77.

Dennett, D.C. (1991) Consciousness Explained. Boston, MA, and London, Little, Brown and Co.

Dennett, D.C. (1995a) Darwin's Dangerous Idea. London, Penguin.

Dennett, D.C. (1995b) The unimagined preposterousness of zombies. Journal of Consciousness Studies 2(4), 322-6.

Dennett, D.C. (1995c) Cog: steps towards consciousness in robots. In T. Metzinger (ed.) Conscious Experience. Thorverton, Devon, Imprint Academic, 471-87.

Dennett, D.C. (1995d) The path not taken. Behavioral and Brain Sciences 18, 252-3; commentary on N. Block, On a confusion about a function of consciousness. Behavioral and Brain Sciences 18, 227.

Dennett, D.C. (1996a) Facing backwards on the problem of consciousness. Journal of Consciousness Studies 3(1), 4-6.

Dennett, D.C. (1996b) Kinds of Minds: Towards an Understanding of Consciousness. London, Weidenfeld & Nicolson.

Dennett, D.C. (1997) An exchange with Daniel Dennett. In J. Searle (ed.) The Mystery of Consciousness. New York, New York Review of Books, 115-19.

Dennett, D.C. (1998) The myth of double transduction. In S.R. Hameroff, A.W. Kaszniak and A. C. Scott (eds) Toward a Science of Consciousness: The Second Tucson Discussions and Debates. Cambridge, MA, MIT Press, 97-107.

Dennett, D.C. (1998b) Brainchildren: Essays on Designing Minds. Cambridge, MA, MIT Press.

Dennett, D.C. (2001) The fantasy of first person science. Debate with D. Chalmers, Northwestern University, Evanston, IL, February 2001.

Dennett, D.C. (2003) Freedom Evolves. New York, Penguin.

Dennett, D.C. and Kinsbourne, M. (1992) Time and the observer: the where and when of consciousness in the brain. Behavioral and Brain Sciences 15, 183-247, including commentaries and authors' responses.

Dewey J., (1911 [1977]), "Epistemological Realism: The Alleged Ubiquity of the Knowledge Relation." Journal of Philosophy, VIII, 20 (September 28, 1911).

Dewhurst, Kenneth, and A. W. Beard. "Sudden Religious Conversions in Temporal Lobe Epilepsy." British Journal of Psychiatry 117 (1970)

Dewhurst K, Beard AW. Sudden religious conversions in temporal lobe epilepsy. 1970 Epilepsy Behav 2003

Devinsky O, Lai G. Spirituality and religion in epilepsy. Epilepsy Behav 2008.

Devinsky, O., Morrell, MJ, Vogt, BA. (1995) 'Contribution of anterior cingulate cortex to behavior', Brain, 118.

Douglas Stone A., Chapter 24, The Indian Comet, in the book Einstein and the Quantum, Princeton University Press, Princeton, New Jersey, 2013.

E. Horvitz, "One Hundred Year Study on Artificial Intelligence: Reflections and Framing," ed: Stanford University, 2014.

Einstein A. (1925). "Quantentheorie des einatomigen idealen Gases". Sitzungsberichte der Preussischen Akademie der Wissenschaften.

Eckhart Meister, Selected Writings

Egidi R., ed. (1999), "Von Wright and 'Dante's Dream': Stages in a Philosophical Pilgrim's Progress", in In Search of a New Humanism: the Philosophy of G.H. von Wright, ed. by R. Egidi, Kluwer, Dordrecht.

Fadiga L, Fogassi L, Pavesi G, Rizzolatti G (1995) Motor facilitation during action observation: a magnetic stimulation study. J Neurophysiol 73: 2608–2611.

Fogassi L, Gallese V, Fadiga L, Rizzolatti G (1998) Neurons responding to the sight of goal directed hand/arm actions in the parietal area PF (7b) of the macaque monkey. Soc Neurosci Abs 24:257.5.

Frith U, Frith CD (2003) Development and neurophysiology of mentalizing. Philos Trans R Soc Lond B Biol Sci 358: 459.

Farah, M.J. (1989), 'The neural basis of mental imagery', Trends in Neurosciences, 10.

Finlay BL, Darlington RB (1995) Linked regularities in the development and evolution of mammalian brains. Science 268.

Freud, S. "The Interpretation of Dreams", 1900

Freud, S. "Selected papers on hysteria and other psychoneuroses" Journal of Nervous and Mental Disease 1909.

Freud, S. "The Origin and Development of Psychoanalysis", 1910

Freud, S. "Psychopathology of everyday life", 1914

Freud, S. "Beyond the Pleasure Principle", 1920

Frith, C.D. & Dolan, R.J. (1997), 'Abnormal beliefs: Delusions and memory', Paper presented at the May,

1997, Harvard Conference on Memory and Belief.

Gay, Volney, ed. Neuroscience and Religion. Plymouth, UK: Lexington Books, 2009.

Gazzaniga, M. S. (1985). The social brain. New York: Basic Books.

Gazzaniga, M.S. (1993), 'Brain mechanisms and conscious experience', Ciba Foundation Symposium, 174.

Geschwind N. "Behavioural changes in temporal lobe epilepsy". Psychol Med. 1979.

Gellhorn, E., Kiely, W.F. "Mystical states of consciousness: neurophysiological and clinical aspects." J Nerv Ment Dis. 1972;154:399-405.

Gilbert SL, Dobyns WB, Lahn BT (2005) Genetic links between brain development and brain evolution. Nat Rev Genet 6.

Gray JA. The Psychology of Fear and Stress. 2nd ed. New York, NY: Cambridge University Press; 1988.

Gloor, P. (1992), 'Amygdala and temporal lobe epilepsy', in The Amygdala: Neurobiological Aspects of Emotion, Memory and Mental Dysfunction, ed J.P. Aggleton (New York: Wiley-Liss).

Greenspan, S. I. and S. G. Shanker (2004). The first idea: How symbols, language, and intelligence evolved from our early primate ancestors to modern humans. Cambridge, MA: Da Capo Press.

Grady, D. (1993), 'The vision thing: Mainly in the brain', Discover, June.

Gallagher HL, Frith CD (2003) Functional imaging of 'theory of mind'. Trends Cogn Sci 7: 77.

Gallese V, Fogassi L, Fadiga L, Rizzolatti G (2002) Action representation and the inferior parietal lobule. In: Prinz W, Hommel B (eds) Attention & Performance XIX. Common mechanisms in perception and action. Oxford University Press, Oxford.

Gallese V, Keysers C, Rizzolatti G (2004) A unifying view of the basis of social cognition. Trends Cogn Sci 8: 396–403.

Gangitano M, Mottaghy FM, Pascual-Leone A (2001) Phase specific modulation of cortical motor output during movement observation. NeuroReport 12: 1489–1492.

Gangitano M, Mottaghy FM, Pascual-Leone A (2004) Modulation of premotor mirror neuron activity during observation of unpredictable grasping movements. Eur J Neurosci 20: 2193– 2202.

Goldman AI, Sripada CS (2004) Simulationist models of face-based emotion recognition. Cognition 94: 193–213.

Grèzes J, Costes N, Decety J (1998) Top-down effect of strategy on the perception of human biological motion: a PET investigation. Cogn Neuropsychol 15: 553–582.

Grèzes J, Armony JL, Rowe J, Passingham RE (2003) Activations related to "mirror" and "canonical" neurones in the human brain: an fMRI study. Neuroimage 18: 928–937.

Gross CG, Rocha-Miranda CE, Bender DB (1972) Visual properties of neurons in the inferotemporal cortex of the macaque. J Neurophysiol 35: 96–111.

Hari R, Forss N, Avikainen S, Kirveskari S, Salenius S, Rizzolatti G (1998) Activation of human primary motor cortex during action observation: a neuromagnetic study.

Proc. Natl Acad Sci USA 95: 15061–15065.

Hardy, G. H. (1940). Ramanujan. Cambridge: Cambridge University Press.

Hall, Daniel, Keith Meador, and Harold Koenig. "Measuring Religiousness in Health Research: Review and Critique." Journal of Religion and Health 47, no. 2 (2008)

Harris, Sam, Jonas Kaplan, Ashley Curiel, Susan Bookheimer, Marco Iacoboni, and Mark Cohen. "The Neural Correlates of Religious and Nonreligious Belief." PLoS One 4, no. 10 (October 1, 2009)

Halgren, E. (1992), 'Emotional neurophysiology of the amygdala within the context of human cognition', in The Amygdala: Neurobiological Aspects of Emotion, Memory and Mental Dysfunction, ed J.P. Aggleton (New York: Wiley-Liss).

Halligan PW, Fink GR, Marshal JC, Vallar G. 2003. Spatial cognition: evidence from visual neglect. Trends Cogn Sci.

Handbook of Emotions, Edited by Michael Lewis, Jeannette M. Haviland-Jones, and Lisa Feldman Barrett, The Guilford Press; 3rd edition (2010).

Haggard, P., Clark, S. and Kalogeras,]. (2002) Voluntary action and conscious awareness, Nature Neuroscience 5, 382-5. Haggard, P., Newman, C. and Magno, E. (1999) On the perceived time of voluntary actions. British Journal of Psychology 90, 291-303.

Hameroff, S.R. and Penrose, R. (1996) Conscious events as orchestrated space-time selections. Journal of Consciousness Studies 3(1), 36-53; also reprinted in J. Shear (ed.) (1997) Explaining Consciousness-The Hard Problem. Cambridge, MA, MIT Press, 177-95.

Hardcastle, V.G. (2000) How to understand theN in NCC. InT. Metzinger (ed.) Neural Correlates of Consciousness. Cambridge, MA, MIT Press, 259-64.

Harding, D.E. (1961) On Having no Head: Zen and the Re-Discovery of the Obvious. London, Buddhist Society.

Hardy, A. (1979) The Spiritual Nature of Man: A Study of Contemporary Religious Experience. Oxford, Clarendon Press.

Hamad, S. (1990) The symbol grounding problem. Physica D 42, 335-46.

Hamad, S. (2001) No easy way out. The Sciences 41(2), 36-42.

Harre, R. and Gillett, G. (1994) The Discursive Mind. Thousand Oaks, CA, Sage.

Haugeland, J. (ed.) (1997) Mind Design II: Philosophy, Psychology, Artificial

Intelligence. Cambridge, MA, MIT Press.

Hauser, M.D. (2000) Wild Minds: What Animals Really Think. New York, Henry Holt and Co.; London, Penguin.

Hearne, K. (1990) The Dream Machine. Northants, Aquarian.

Hebb, D.O. (1949) The Organization of Behavior. New York, Wiley.

Helmholtz, H.L.F. von (1856-67) Treatise on Physiological Optics.

Hess, EH (1975) "The role of pupil size in communication," Scientific American, 233(5), 110–12.

Heyes, C.M. (1998) Theory of mind in nonhuman primates. Behavioral and Brain Sciences 21, 101-48; with commentaries.

Heyes, C.M. and Galef, B.G. (eds) (1996) Social Learning in Animals: The Roots of Culture. San Diego, CA, Academic Press.

Hilgard, E.R. (1986) Divided Consciousness: Multiple Controls in Human Thought and Action. New York, Wiley.

Hocquette JF (2016) Is in vitro meat the solution for the future? Meat Science 120: 167–176

Hodgson, R. (1891) A case of double consciousness. Proceedings of the Society for Psychical Research 7, 221-58.

Hofstadter, D.R. (1979) Code!, Escher, Bach: An Eternal Golden Braid. London, Penguin.

Hofstadter, D.R. and Dennett, D.C. (eds) (1981) The Mind's I: Fantasies and Reflections on Self and Soul. London, Penguin.

Holland, J. (ed.) (2001) Ecstasy: The Complete Guide: A Comprehensive Look at the Risks and Benefits of

MDMA. Rochester, VT, Park Street Press.

Holmes, D.S. (1987) The influence of meditation versus rest on physiological arousal. In M. West (ed.) The Psychology of Meditation. Oxford, Clarendon Press, 81-103.

Holt, J. (1999) Blindsight in debates about qualia. Journal of Consciousness Studies 6(5), 54-71.

Horgan, J. (1994), 'Can science explain consciousness?', Scientific American, 271.

Holloway RL (1996) Evolution of the human brain. In: Lock A, Peters CR (eds) Handbook of human symbolic evolution. Oxford University Press, Oxford

Iacoboni M, Woods RP, Brass M, Bekkering H, Mazziotta JC, Rizzolatti G (1999) Cortical mechanisms of human imitation. Science 286: 2526-2528.

Iacoboni M, Koski LM, Brass M, Bekkering H, Woods RP, Dubeau MC, Mazziotta JC, Rizzolatti G (2001) Reafferent copies of imitated actions in the right superior temporal cortex. Proc Natl Acad Sci USA 98: 13995–13999.

Jeannerod M (1988) The neural and behavioural organization of goal-directed movements. Clarendon Press, Oxford.

Johnson-Frey SH, Maloof FR, Newman-Norlund R, Farrer C, Inati S, Grafton ST (2003) Actions or hand-objects interactions? Human inferior frontal cortex and action observation. Neuron 39: 1053–1058.

Jackson, F. (1982) Epiphenomenal qualia. Philosophical Quarterly 32, 127-36.

James, W. (1890) The Principles of Psychology (2 volumes). London, Macmillan.

James, W. (1902) The Varieties of Religious Experience: A Study in Human Nature. New York and London, Longmans, Green and Co.

Jansen, K. (2001) Ketamine: Dreams and Realities. Sarasota, FL, Multidisciplinary Association for Psychedelic Studies.

Jay, M. (ed.) (1999) Artificial Paradises: A Drugs Reader. London, Penguin.

Jaynes, J. (1976) The Origin of Consciousness in the Breakdown of the Bicameral Mind. New York, Houghton Mifflin.

Johnson, M.K. and Raye, C.L. (1981) Reality monitoring. Psychological Review 88, 67-85.

Kadim I, Mahgoub O, Baqir S et al. (2015) Cultured meat from muscle stem cells: a review of challenges and prospects. J Integr Agr 14: 222–233

Koski L, Iacoboni M, Dubeau MC, Woods RP, Mazziotta JC (2003) Modulation of cortical activity during different imitative behaviors. J Neurophysiol 89: 460–471.

Krolak-Salmon P, Henaff MA, Isnard J, Tallon-Baudry C, Guenot M, Vighetto A, Bertrand O, Mauguiere F (2003) An attention modulated response to disgust in human ventral anterior insula. Ann Neurol 53: 446–453.

Kandel, E. R. In Search of Memory: The Emergence of a New Science of Mind, W. W. Norton & Company (2007).

Kandel E. R. Schwartz JH, Jessel TM. Principles of neural sciences. New York; McGraw Hill, 2000.

Kanizsa, G. (1979), Organization In Vision (New York: Praeger).

Kaloupek DG, Scott JR, Khatami V. Assessment of coping strategies associated with syncope in blood donors. J Psychosom Res. 1985;29:207-214.

Kanwisher, N. (2001) Neural events and perceptual awareness. Cognition 79, 89-113; also reprinted inS. Dehaene (ed.) The Cognitive Neuroscience of Consciousness. Cambridge, MA, MIT Press, 89-113.

Kapleau, Roshi P. (1980) The Three Pillars of Zen: Teaching, Practice, and Enlightenment (revised edn). New York, Doubleday.

Karn, K. and Hayhoe, M. (2000) Memory representations guide targeting eye movements in a natural task. Visual Cognition 7, 673-703.

Kasamatsu, A. and Hirai, T. (1966) An electroencephalographic study on the Zen meditation (zazen). Folia Psychiatrica et Neurologica Japonica 20, 315-36.

Kaiserman-Abramof, I. R., Graybiel, A. M., & Nauta, W. J. (1980). The thalamic projection to cortical area 17 in a congenitally anophthalmic mouse strain. Neuroscience, 5, 41–52.

Kanold, P. O., Kara, P., Reid, R. C., & Shatz, C. J. (2003). Role of subplate neurons in functional maturation of visual cortical columns. Science, 301, 521–525.

Kennedy, H., & Dehay, C. (1988). Functional implications of the anatomical organization of the callosal projections of visual areas V1 and V2 in the macaque monkey. Behav. Brain Res., 29, 225–236.

Kentridge, R.W. and Heywood, C.A. (1999) The status of blindsight. Journal of Consciousness Studies 6(5), 3-11.

Kihlstrom, J.F. (1996) Perception without awareness of what is perceived, learning without awareness of what is learned. In M. Velmans (ed.) The Science of Consciousness. London, Routledge, 23-46.

Kollerstrom, N. (1999) The path of Halley's comet, and Newton's late apprehension of the law of gravity. Annals of Science 56, 331-56.

Kosslyn, S.M. (1980) Image and Mind. Cambridge, MA, Harvard University Press.

Kosslyn, S.M. (1988) Aspects of a cognitive neuroscience of mental imagery. Science 240, 1621-6.

Kinsbourne, M. (1995), 'The intralaminar thalamic nucleii', Consciousness and Cognition, 4.

Kjaer, Troels, Camilla Bertelsen, Paola Piccini, David Brooks, Jorgen Alving, and Hans Lou. "Increased Dopamine Tone during Meditation- Induced Change of Consciousness." Cognitive Brain Research 13, no. 2 (April 2002)

Kölmel HW. 1985. Complex visual hallucinations in the hemianopic field. J Neurol Neurosurg Psychiatry.

Koenig, Harold. "Research on Religion, Spirituality, and Mental Health: A Review." Canadian Journal of Psychiatry 54, no. 5 (May 2009)

Koenig, Harold, ed. Handbook of Religion and Mental Health. San Diego, CA: Academic Press, 1998

Kraepelin E. Psychiatry: A Textbook for Students and Physicians. New York, NY: Science History Publications; 1990.

Lauglin, Charles, John McManus, and Eugene d'Aquili. Brain, Symbol, and Experience. 2nd ed. New York: Columbia University Press, 1992

Lakoff, G. and M. Johnson (1999). Philosophy in the flesh. Basic Books: New York.

LeDoux, J. E. (1996). The emotional brain. New York: Simon & Schuster.

LeDoux, J.E. (1992), 'Emotion and the amygdala', in The Amygdala:

Neurobiological Aspects of Emo- tion, Memory and Mental Dysfunction, ed J.P. Aggleton (New York: Wiley-Liss).

Levin, D.T. and Simons, D.J. (1997) Failure to detect changes to attended objects in motion pictures. Psychonomic Bulletin and Review 4, 501-6.

Levine,J. (1983) Materialism and qualia: the explanatory gap. Pacific Philosophical Quarterly 64, 354-61.

Levine,J. (2001) Purple Haze: The Puzzle of Consciousness. New York, Oxford University Press. Levine, S. (1979) A Gradual Awakening. New York, Doubleday.

Levinson, B.W. (1965) States of awareness during general anaesthesia. British Journal of Anaesthesia 37, 544-6.

Lewicki, P., Czyzewska, M. and Hoffman, H. (1987) Unconscious acquisition of complex procedural knowledge. Journal of Experimental Psychology: Learning, Memory and Cognition 13, 523-30.

Lewicki, P., Hill, T. and Bizot, E. (1988) Acquisition of procedural knowledge about a pattern of stimuli that cannot be articulated. Cognitive Psychology 20, 24-37.

Lewicki, P., Hill, T. and Czyzewska, M. (1992) Nonconscious acquisition of information. American Psychologist 47, 796-801.

Manthey S, Schubotz RI, von Cramon DY (2003). Premotor cortex in observing erroneous action: an fMRI study. Brain Res Cogn Brain Res 15: 296–307.

Mesulam MM, Mufson EJ (1982) Insula of the old world monkey. III: Efferent cortical output and comments on function. J Comp Neurol 212: 38–52.

Naskar, Abhijit. "Homo: A Brief History of Consciousness", 2015

Naskar, Abhijit. "What is Mind?", 2016

Naskar, Abhijit. "In Search of Divinity: Journey to The Kingdom of Conscience", 2016

Naskar, Abhijit. "Love, God & Neurons: Memoir of A Scientist who found himself by getting lost", 2016

Naskar, Abhijit. "Neurons of Jesus: Mind of A Teacher, Spouse & Thinker", 2017

Naskar, Abhijit. "Principia Humanitas", 2017

Naskar, Abhijit. "We Are All Black: A Treatise on Racism", 2017

Naskar, Abhijit. "Wise Mating: A Treatise on Monogamy", 2017

Naskar, Abhijit. "Illusion of Religion: A Treatise on Religious Fundamentalism", 2017

Naskar, Abhijit. "I Am The Thread: My Mission", 2017

Naskar, Abhijit. "Morality Absolute", 2017

Naskar, Abhijit. "Build Bridges not Walls: In the name of Americana", 2018

Naskar, Abhijit. "Fabric of Humanity", 2018

Naskar, Abhijit. "Lives To Serve Before I Sleep", 2019

Naskar, Abhijit. "The Constitution of The United Peoples of Earth", 2019

Naskar, Abhijit. "Neurons Giveth, Neurons Taketh Away | Abhijit Naskar | TEDxIIMRanchi", 2019 https://www.youtube.com/watch?v=B NX-Q0ySm80

Naskar, Abhijit. "Mission Reality", 2019

Naskar, Abhijit. "Operation Justice: To Make A Society That Needs No Law", 2019

Newberg, Andrew, and Jeremy Iversen. "The Neural Basis of the Complex Mental Task of Meditation: Neurotransmitter and Neurochemical Considerations." Medical Hypotheses 61, no. 2 (2003).

Newberg, Andrew. "How God Changes Your Brain: An Introduction to Jewish Neurotheology", CCAR Journal: The Reform Jewish Quarterly, Winter 2016.

Newberg, Andrew, and Stephanie Newberg. "A Neuropsychological Perspective on Spiritual Development." In Handbook of Spiritual Development in Childhood and Adolescence, edited by Eugene Roehlkepartain, Pamela King, Linda Wagener, and Peter Benson. London: Sage Publications, Inc., 2005

Newberg, Andrew. "The Neurotheology Link An Intersection Between Spirituality and Health",

Alternative and Complimentary Therapies, Vol 21 No 1, February 2015.

Newberg, Andrew, Nancy Wintering, Dharma Khalsa, Hannah Roggenkamp, and Mark Waldman. "Meditation Effects on Cognitive Function and Cerebral Blood Flow in Subjects with Memory Loss: A Preliminary Study." Journal of Alzheimer's Disease 20, no. 2 (2010)

Nash, M. (1995), 'Glimpses of the mind', Time.

Nesse RM. Proximate and evolutionary studies of anxiety, stress and depression: synergy at the interface. Neurosci Biobehav Rev. 1999;23:895-903.

Nicolelis, Miguel. (2011) "Beyond Boundaries: The New Neuroscience of Connecting Brains with Machines---and How It Will Change Our Lives", Times Books

O'Hara, K. and Scutt, T. (1996) There is no hard problem of consciousness. Journal of Consciousness Studies 3(4), 290-302, reprinted in J. Shear (ed.) (1997) Explaining Consciousness. Cambridge, MA, MIT Press, 69-82.

O'Regan, J.K. (1992) Solving the "real" mysteries of visual perception: the world as an outside memory. Canadian Journal of Psychology 46, 461-88.

O'Regan, J.K. and Noe, A. (2001) A sensorimotor account of vision and visual consciousness. Behavioral and Brain Sciences 24(5), 883-917.

O'Regan, J.K., Rensink, R.A. and Clark,].]. (1999) Change-blindness as a result of "mudsplashes." Nature 398, 34.

Ornstein, R.E. (1977) The Psychology of Consciousness (2nd edn). New York, Harcourt.

Ornstein, R.E. (1986) The Psychology of Consciousness (3rd edn). New York, Pehguin.

Ornstein, R.E. (1992) The Evolution of Consciousness. New York, Touchstone.

Penfield W, Faulk ME (1955) The insula: further observations on its function. Brain 78: 445– 470.

Penrose, R. (1994), Shadows of the Mind (Oxford: Oxford University Press).

Penrose, R. (1989), The Emperor's New Mind: Concerning Computers, Minds and The Laws of Physics (Oxford: Oxford University Press).

Persinger, "'I would kill in God's name' role of sex, weekly church attendance, report of a religious experience and limbic lability" Perceptual and Motor Skills 1997.

Persinger "Experimental simulation of the God experience" Neurotheology 2003.

Persinger, M. A. (1993b). Personality changes following brain injury as a grief response to the loss of sense of self: Phenomenological themes as indices of local lability and neurocognitive restructuring as psycho- therapy. Psychological Reports, 72

Persinger, Corradini, Clement, Keaney, et al "Neurotheology and its convergence with neuroquantology" NeuroQuantology 2010.

Persinger, Koren and St-Pierre "The electromagnetic induction of mystical and altered states within the laboratory" Journal of Consciousness Exploration and Research 2010.

Persinger "Case report: A prototypical spontaneous 'sensed presence' of a sentient being and concomitant electroencephalographic activity in the clinical laboratory" Neurocase 2008.

Persinger and Saroka "Potential production of Hughlings Jackson's "parasitic consciousness" by physiologically-patterned weak transcerebral magnetic fields: QEEG and source localization" Epilepsy & Behavior 28 (2013).

Persinger. "The neuropsychiatry of paranormal experiences". J Neuropsychiatry Clin Neurosci 2001.

Persinger. "Neuropsychological bases of god beliefs", New York: Praeger, 1987

Persinger. "Temporal lobe epileptic signs and correlative behaviors displayed by normal populations", Journal of General Psychology, 1986

Perry BD, Pollard R. Homeostasis, stress, trauma, and adaptation. A neurodevelopmental view of childhood trauma. Child Adolesc Psychiatr Clin N Am. 1998;7:33.

Paré, D. & Llinás, R. (1995), 'Conscious and preconscious processes as seen from the standpoint of sleep-waking cycle neurophysiology', Neuropsychologia, 33.

P. S. de Laplace. Essai Philosophique sur les Probabilites [1814], in Academy des Sciences, Oeuvres Complotes de Laplace, Vol. 7, Gauthier-Villars, Paris (1886).

Perrett DI, Harries MH, Bevan R, Thomas S, Benson PJ, Mistlin AJ, Chitty AJ, Hietanen JK, Ortega JE (1989) Frameworks of analysis for the neural representation of animate objects and actions. J Exp Bio 146: 87–113.

Phillips ML, Young AW, Senior C, Brammer M, Andrew C, Calder AJ, Bullmore ET, Perrett DI, Rowland D, Williams SC, Gray JA, David AS (1997)

A specific neural substrate for perceiving facial expressions of disgust. Nature 389: 495–498.

Phillips ML, Young AW, Scott SK, Calder AJ, Andrew C, Giampietro V, Williams SC, Bullmore ET, Brammer M, Gray JA (1998) Neural responses to facial and vocal expressions of fear and disgust. Proc R Soc Lond B Biol Sci 265: 1809–1817.

Puce A, Perrett D (2003) Electrophysiological and brain imaging of biological motion. Philosoph Trans Royal Soc Lond, Series B, 358: 435–445.

Ramachandran VS. Behavioral and magnetoencephalographic correlates of plasticity in the adult human brain. Proc Natl Acad Sci USA 1993; 90: 10413–20.

Ramachandran VS. Phantom limbs, neglect syndromes, repressed memories, and Freudian psychology. Int Rev Neurobiol 1994; 37: 291–333.

Ramachandran VS. Plasticity and functional recovery in neurology. Clin Med 2005; 5: 368–73.

Ramachandran VS, Hirstein W. The perception of phantom limbs. The D. O. Hebb lecture. Brain 1998; 121: 1603–30.

Ramachandran VS, Rogers-Ramachandran D, Cobb S. Touching the phantom limb. Nature 1995; 377: 489–90.

Ramachandran VS, Rogers-Ramachandran D. Phantom limbs and neural plasticity. Arch Neurol 2000; 57: 317–20.

Ramachandran VS, Rogers-Ramachandran D. It's all done with mirrors. Sci Am Mind 2007; 18: 16–9.

Ramachandran VS, Rogers-Ramachandran D. Sensations referred

to a patient's phantom arm from another subjects intact arm: perceptual correlates of mirror neurons. Med Hypotheses 2008; 70: 1233–4.

Ramachandran VS, Rogers-Ramachandran D, Stewart M. Perceptual correlates of massive cortical reorganization. Science 1992; 258: 1159–60.

Rizzolatti G, Craighero L (2004) The mirror-neuron system. Annu Rev Neurosci 27: 169–192.

Rizzolatti G, Fogassi L, Gallese V (2001) Neurophysiological mechanisms underlying the understanding and imitation of action. Nature Rev Neurosci 2:661–670.

Rock I, Victor J. Vision and touch: an experimentally created conflict between the two senses. Science 1964; 143: 594–6.

Rose´n B, Lundborg G. Training with a mirror in rehabilitation of the hand.

Scand J Plast Reconstr Surg Hand Surg 2005; 39: 104–8.

Royet JP, Plailly J, Delon-Martin C, Kareken DA, Segebarth C (2003) fMRI of emotional responses to odors: influence of hedonic valence and judgment, handedness, and gender. Neuroimage 20: 713–728.

Rozin R Haidt J and McCauley CR (2000) Disgust. In: Lewis M, Haviland-Jones JM (eds) Handbook of Emotion. 2nd Edition. Guilford Press, New York, pp 637–653.

Saxe R, Carey S, Kanwisher N (2004) Understanding other minds: linking developmental psychology and functional neuroimaging. Annu Rev Psychol 55: 87–124.

S. J. Russell and P. Norvig, Artificial intelligence: a modern approach (3rd edition): Prentice Hall, 2009.

Schienle A, Stark R, Walter B, Blecker C, Ott U, Kirsch P, Sammer G, Vaitl D

(2002) The insula is not specifically involved in disgust processing: an fMRI study. Neuroreport 13: 2023–2026.

Showers MJC, Lauer EW (1961) Somatovisceral motor patterns in the insula. J Comp Neurol 117: 107–115.

Singer T, Seymour B, O'Doherty J, Kaube H, Dolan RJ, Frith CD (2004) Empathy for pain involves the affective but not the sensory components of pain. Science 303: 1157–1162.

Smith A (1759) The theory of moral sentiments (ed. 1976). Clarendon Press, Oxford.

S. N. Bose (1924). "Plancks Gesetz und Lichtquantenhypothese". Zeitschrift für Physik. 26 (1): 178–181.

Sprengelmeyer R, Rausch M, Eysel UT, Przuntek H (1998) Neural structures associated with recognition of facial expressions of basic emotions Proc R Soc Lond B Biol Sci 265: 1927–1931.

Strafella AP, Paus T (2000) Modulation of cortical excitability during action observation: a transcranial magnetic stimulation study. NeuroReport 11: 2289–2292.

Simonsen R (2015) Eating for the future: veganism and the challenge of in vitro meat. In: Stapleton P, Byers A (Hg). Biopolitics and utopia. Palgrave Macmillan, New York (2015), S 167–190

Tanaka K (1996) Inferotemporal cortex and object vision. Ann Rev Neurosci. 19: 109–140.

Tesla N. "My Inventions", 1919

T. R. Society, "Machine learning: the power and promise of computers that learn by example," ed. The Royal Society, 2017.

Tomasello M, Call J (1997) Primate cognition. Oxford University Press, Oxford.

Tremblay C, Robert M, Pascual-Leone A, Lepore F, Nguyen DK, Carmant L, Bouthillier A, Theoret H (2004) Action observation and execution: intracranial recordings in a human subject. Neurology. 63: 937–938.

Umilta MA, Kohler E, Gallese V, Fogassi L, Fadiga L, Keysers C, Rizzolatti G (2001) "I know what you are doing": a neurophysiological study. Neuron 32: 91–101.

Von Wright G.H., (1963), Norm and Action. A Logical Inquiry, Routledge & Kegan Paul, London.

Von Wright G.H., (1976), "Determinism and the Study of Man", in Essays on Explanation and Understanding, ed. by J. Manninen and R. Tuomela, Reidel, Dordrecht.

Von Wright G.H., (1977), "What is Humanism?", The Lindlay Lecture, University of Arkansas, Lawrence, Kansas.

Von Wright G.H., (1979), "Humanism and the Humanities", in Philosophy and Grammar, ed. by S. Kanger and S. Öhman, Reidel, Dordrecht, pp. 1-16. Reprinted in von Wright (1993).

Von Wright G.H., (1980), Freedom and Determination, North-Holland Publishing Co., Amsterdam.

Von Wright G.H., (1985), Of Human Freedom, The Tanner Lectures on Human Values,

Vol. VI, ed. by S. M. McMurrin, University of Utah Press, Salt Lake City, pp. 107-70. Reprinted in von Wright (1998).

Von Wright G.H., (1993), The Tree of Knowledge and Other Essays, Brill, Leiden.

Von Wright G.H., (1997), "Progress: Fact and Fiction", in The Idea of Progress, ed. by A. Burgen et al., W. de Gruyter, Berlin, pp. 1-18.

Von Wright G.H., (1998), In the Shadow of Descartes: Essays in the Philosophy of Mind, Kluwer, Dordrecht.